ME: FACTS AND FORECASTS

A GUIDE FOR NOW AND LATER

WRITTEN BY YOU

WITH HELP FROM AMY K. ATCHA

ME: FACTS AND FORECASTS

A GUIDE FOR NOW AND LATER

ME: Facts and Forecasts, A Guide for Now and Later
By Amy K. Atcha
Copyright 2011 Customized Caring, Inc.

Artwork and cover by Michael Telapary
http://www.tewanka.com

Design and composition by Christopher Lake
http://www.cmlstudios.com

Published by Customized Caring Publishing
ISBN-13: 978-0615531878

For information about special discounts for bulk purchases, please contact Customized Caring at 630.306.4480 or www.customizedcaring.com.

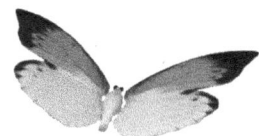

FIRST AND FOREMOST

Last Name		First Name	Middle Initial
Gender	Date of Birth	Weight	Blood Type
Language spoken			
Address			
City		State	Zip Code
Primary Insurance Co.		Primary Insurance Number & Group	
Secondary Insurance Co.		Secondary Insurance Number & Group	
Medicare?		Social Security Number	

Primary Doctor's Name		Phone Number	
Address			
City		State	Zip Code

Allergies to medications and food:

_____

_____

_____

Emergency Contact's Name	Phone Number	
Relationship		
Address		
City	State	Zip Code

SPECIAL INSTRUCTIONS

DO NOT RESUSCITATE (DNR)?

Yes ☐   No ☐

LIFE SUPPORT

I DO want the following Life Support systems

☐ Feeding tube / nutritional therapy

☐ Medication therapy

☐ Oxygen therapy / Respirator

Signature _____

Date _____

I have a Power of Attorney for Health Care Matters

Yes ☐   No ☐

Relevant documents are located in:

_____

_____

I have Advanced Directives for Healthcare

Yes ☐   No ☐

Relevant documents are located in:

_____

_____

Power of Attorney		Phone Number	
Address			
City		State	Zip Code
Email Address			

I have a Legal Guardian:

Yes ☐   No ☐

The Guardian is for my:

Estate ☐   Person ☐   Both ☐

Relevant Court documents are located in:

_____

_____

Legal Guardian – Estate	Phone Number	
Address		
City	State	Zip Code

Legal Guardian – Person	Phone Number	
Address		
City	State	Zip Code

DEDICATION

This book is dedicated to all of us who have ever "stepped into the shoes" of someone we love. A special thanks to my late brother Jeff and my grandparents Katie and Lyle Brundage and Mary and Henry Arcy, for giving me the joy of helping you, in good times and in bad, in this life and beyond. The experience of sharing your lives at such critical moments brought insight, inspiration and purpose to my life. A special thanks to my brothers Dan and Matt for your patience and love; and to Mom and Dad also for your constant love, support and encouragement. Finally, to my husband, Iqbal, and my daughter Kim, for sharing the efforts of this book and the events in life that precipitated it. You will all forever be in my heart.

ME: Facts and Forecasts

PREFACE

One day he was fine. The next he was in a coma. During the following six years, he was in and out of a state of dementia, confusion and disorientation. Seeing my brother go from a thriving self-sufficient adult to a confused, almost child-like man, I learned the hard way that a competent life is a gift.

At the age of 42, my brother Jeff was the epitome of independence. He had a good job, financial security, a home in which he lived alone. He drove, shopped, traveled, and cared for himself. Suddenly, all things changed.

As with many of us, Jeff's health was not the best — perhaps it was his lifestyle, or maybe it was just fate itself. When he came out of the coma, his life was changed forever. At first, when he couldn't communicate or care for himself, I chalked it up to the heart attack and resulting lack of oxygen. Like most family members, I figured he would take that long, slow path to a full (or almost full) recovery. But that wasn't the case.

As the days went on, I began to think — this could take a while. So I asked Mom and Dad: Who's going to take care of Jeff's house? Pay his bills? Pick up his mail? Since he was over

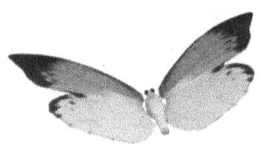

the age of 18, not married and had no children, someone would need to be appointed to manage his business affairs. Having worked with the federal court system in my "day job," and since I am an accountant, I offered to Mom and Dad that I would pick up the pieces. They agreed.

So off to court we went. Since Jeff had not appointed a Power of Attorney for his financial affairs nor provided any Advanced Directives for Healthcare, and since he was not, at that time, competent to select anyone to help, the state court would need to intervene. After a brief hearing with a judge, and of course after all the requisite paperwork had been completed — I was appointed as Jeff's Legal Guardian. I was then legally responsible for my brother's life — both his body (medical care) and his assets.

That's when the full scope of what had just happened set in. What did I really know about my brother? Did he have health insurance? Where was the key to his mailbox?

I had to learn the hard way, how to pick up the pieces of someone else's life. Although I could get into his house and even had his wallet, I still had no idea how he typically lived. How did he get paid — by check? Or by electronic deposit? Where did he have his bank accounts? How did he pay his bills... and what bills did he even have to pay?!

Then, of course, there was the even more personal side — what if he had another heart attack? Would he want to be resuscitated? And what happens if, and when, he died? Did he have a will? If so, where was it?

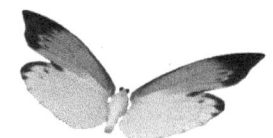

All these questions, and more, were circling inside my head — and all of this at a time when his life was still hanging by a thread. Decisions had to be made and life still had to go on... with me picking up the pieces as best I could.

Needless to say, I managed — with the help and support of family, friends and advisors — but it made me realize... it all could have been much easier, if only he had been organized and prepared for these unpleasant times.

Let's face it — we'll all be in this, or a similar, situation one day — that's life. And how many of us are prepared?

So my request to you is this — sit with your family, discuss these matters, use this book and feel the power and weight lifted from the shoulders of all to live the rest of your days (and perhaps theirs) with the knowledge that you care enough to ease your life and theirs for all your days to come.

ME: FACTS AND FORECASTS

INTRODUCTION

What if something happened to you — and someone had to "step into your shoes" — whether for a month, a year or the rest of your life?

What if you couldn't communicate, even for a short period of time?

What if you couldn't care for yourself?

Worse yet, what if this happened and you weren't prepared?

Who would you want to pick up the pieces, if even only on a temporary basis? Who is that person? Do you know? And more importantly — does he/she?

Would that person know where you kept your legal documents? What bills to expect to pay? What income to be collecting for you?

And what about those tough decisions — the final decisions of your life — would that person know what you want? Does that person know what your beliefs are, what your wishes were?

An illness, or worse, can be a challenging time — emotionally draining, stressful, physically exhausting. For most of us,

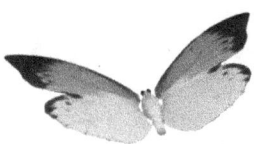

we think we are either going to be alive or dead — rarely does anyone ever contemplate another alternative. But what if?

This book assembles the many pieces of your full and complex life into one short workbook. The idea is to consolidate the information so that if something did happen to you, your family, a close friend, or even a Power of Attorney or Legal Guardian, could step in and help you out — with the least disruption to you and your life and your matters. It also provides a convenient and safe place for you to identify and document your wishes and preferences, in the event that you become disabled and you're not able to care for yourself — either physically or financially.

And finally, what about those important end-of-life decisions — the ones not many of us want to discuss? We each handle things in our own way — so let this book assist you in communicating what is "your way." If you've never had that "uncomfortable" yet very necessary, discussion with your family and friends, then this is your time and your place to leave appropriate information that will be of help.

This workbook is organized into two sections — Facts and Forecasts. At the beginning of each section, some insights are provided to better help you understand the needs and uses of the information.

The Facts are simply that — Facts — about your life as it is right now:

- Who are you?
- Where and how do you live?
- Who are your doctors?

- What insurance do you have?
- Where are your assets held?
- What help do you receive from others?
- How do you spend a typical day?

The Forecasts are your wishes — your choices — for those times when you need help — whether a little or a lot — and in preparation of the life hereafter. If you have a choice:

- Who do you want to help care for you?
- Where do you want to live?
- Who will help you make your decisions?
  - On your health?
  - On your finances?

The last pages are for your legacies:

- How do you want to be remembered?
- What special gifts and blessings do you want to leave behind?

This book gives you the peace of mind that others will know your wishes and better be prepared for when the time comes to use this information. Then, during such a bittersweet time, family and friends can find the joy in your life and celebrate your memories.

Now remember, this is your book about YOU! I'm just helping you write it. You can put in as much, or as little, information as you want — and you can revise it at any time. The more you share, the more your friends and family can help you.

Me: The Facts

Personal Information

Legal Information

Medical Information

Financial Information

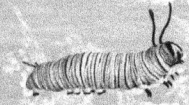

ME: FACTS AND FORECASTS

ME: THE FACTS

PERSONAL INFORMATION

Personal information is, of course, personal. But it is also necessary to function in today's world. No matter where you go, and sometimes what you do, you need to provide personal information — your age, your birthdate, your address, etc.

Due to its importance, almost all of your personal information is protected by various state and federal laws. The release of this information is extremely limited — even to family members. However, for those making an effort to help you, this personal information is critical. Thus there is a need to document certain pieces of information so that others can help you, when emergencies arise.

This section will identify several pieces of basic personal information which may be used to identify you, your daily schedule, who you have designated as your emergency

contacts, your religious and cultural preferences and beliefs. This section also provides a place to list all family members and friends to which you might want to remain in contact or who have information about you that would assist in your care.

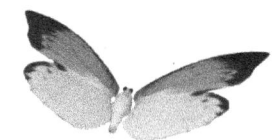

PERSONAL INFORMATION

Nickname/ Preferred Name		
Last Name	First Name	Middle Initial
Languages Spoken		
Address		
City	State	Zip Code
County	Country (if not US)	
Birthdate	Social Security Number	

PHONE NUMBERS AND E-MAIL ADDRESS

Home
Cell / Mobile
Office
E-Mail
Other Contacts

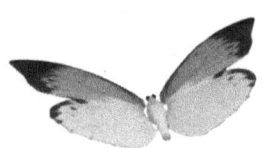

The person who knows most about me is:

_____

I have a passport:	Yes ☐	No ☐
I have a driver's license:	Yes ☐	No ☐
I have a Social Security card:	Yes ☐	No ☐
I have other identification cards:	Yes ☐	No ☐

    These items are located in _____

I have pets: Yes ☐   No ☐

    Animal _____   Name _____

    Animal _____   Name _____

    Animal _____   Name _____

My favorite things (colors, flowers, music, television, movies, best friend, memories, etc.) are:

_____

_____

_____

_____

_____

_____

_____

_____

_____

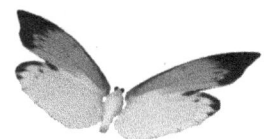

RELIGION

Faith of Choice		
Place of Worship (i.e. church, temple, mosque)		
Name of Clergy/Religious Leader	Phone Number	
Address		
City	State	Zip Code

My Cultural Beliefs and Practices are (i.e., preferences, daily / weekly rituals, avoidances):

_____

_____

_____

_____

_____

My Hobbies and other Interests are:

_____

_____

_____

_____

_____

_____

_____

_____

Things I dislike are:

_____

_____

_____

_____

_____

_____

_____

_____

ME: FACTS AND FORECASTS

I live:

- ☐ by myself
- ☐ with my family
- ☐ with my friends

I live in:

- ☐ a house
- ☐ an apartment / condominium
- ☐ a senior living center or other group housing environment

Emergency Contact Person	Phone Number	
Address		
City	State	Zip Code

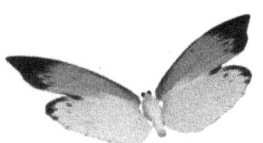

My Family and Relatives

Name	Relationship	Contact Information
Name	Relationship	Contact Information
Name	Relationship	Contact Information
Name	Relationship	Contact Information
Name	Relationship	Contact Information
Name	Relationship	Contact Information
Name	Relationship	Contact Information

MY FRIENDS AND OTHER IMPORTANT PEOPLE

Name	Relationship	Contact Information
Name	Relationship	Contact Information
Name	Relationship	Contact Information
Name	Relationship	Contact Information
Name	Relationship	Contact Information
Name	Relationship	Contact Information
Name	Relationship	Contact Information

MY DAILY SCHEDULE

TIME	MONDAY	TUESDAY	WEDNESDAY	THURSDAY	FRIDAY	SATURDAY	SUNDAY
5:00							
6:00							
7:00							
8:00							
9:00							
10:00							
11:00							
12:00 pm							
1:00							
2:00							
3:00							
4:00							
5:00							
6:00							
7:00							
8:00							
9:00							
10:00							
11:00							
12:00 am							

ME: THE FACTS

LEGAL INFORMATION

A legal document is any formally executed written paper or electronic file, that can be attributed to its author, thatrecords and formally expresses a legally enforceable act or contractual duty, obligation, or right. Legal documents are a part of many of our lives — whether it be with respect to our finances or our physical person. Typical legal documents include Wills, Powers of Attorney and Advanced Directives.

This section provides space for you to identify those basic legal documents which you may have already executed, and should be used to help provide for your care. These documents may be specific to your finances or to your physical person, or both. These agreements and documents typically designate who and when someone is authorized to act on your behalf.

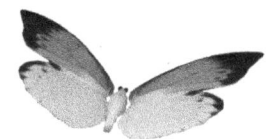

LEGAL INFORMATION

I have a Power of Attorney for Health Care Matters:

Yes ☐   No ☐

Relevant documents are located in:

_____

_____

Power of Attorney – Healthcare	Phone Number	
Address		
City	State	Zip Code

I have Advanced Directives for Healthcare:

Yes ☐   No ☐

Relevant documents are located in:

_____

_____

I have a Power of Attorney for my Financial Affairs:

Yes ☐   No ☐

Relevant documents are located in:

_____

_____

Power of Attorney – Financial	Phone Number	
Address		
City	State	Zip Code

I have a Legal Guardian:

Yes ☐   No ☐

The Guardian is for my:

Estate ☐   Person ☐   Both ☐

Relevant Court papers are located in:

_____

_____

Legal Guardian – Estate	Phone Number	
Address		
City	State	Zip Code

Legal Guardian – Person	Phone Number	
Address		
City	State	Zip Code

I have a Will:

Yes ☐   No ☐

Relevant documents are located in:

_____

_____

Executor of Will		
Name of Firm	Phone Number	
Address		
City	State	Zip Code

Others who have copies of my Will:

_____

_____

_____

_____

Special Instructions regarding legal information:

_____

_____

_____

_____

_____

_____

_____

_____

ME: FACTS AND FORECASTS

ME: THE FACTS

MEDICAL INFORMATION

Medical information is anything that relates to your physical and mental well-being. Your medical history, diagnoses and even medications are private information that are protected by state and federal laws. This information can only be shared with your consent.

This information, however, can also be used to save your life (and from the financial view, your money!).

The following section provides space to identify your insurance carriers, doctors, health conditions and medications, as well as your dental and vision care information. You may also designate who this information may be shared with, or withheld from.

ME: FACTS AND FORECASTS

MEDICAL INFORMATION

My medical information may be released to the following people:

_____

_____

_____

_____

_____ My Initials

My medical information is **not to be released** to the following people:

_____

_____

_____

_____

_____ My Initials

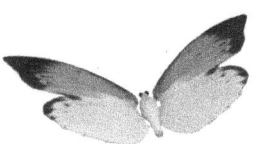

I am covered by Medicare

Yes ☐   No ☐

I am covered by Medicaid

Yes ☐   No ☐

I have private health insurance

Yes ☐   No ☐

I have secondary health insurance

Yes ☐   No ☐

I have Long Term Care insurance

Yes ☐   No ☐

I have separate prescription drug coverage

Yes ☐   No ☐

I usually use a mail order pharmacy

Yes ☐   No ☐

Health Insurance / Medicare /Medicaid Information

Primary Insurance Company	
Policy Number	Group Number
Phone or other contact number	
Responsible Party	

Secondary Insurance Company	
Policy Number	Group Number
Phone or other contact number	
Responsible Party	

Long Term Care Insurance

Insurance Company	
Policy Number	Group Number
Phone or other contact number	
Responsible Party	

Special Instructions regarding Health Insurance:

_____

_____

_____

_____

_____

_____

_____

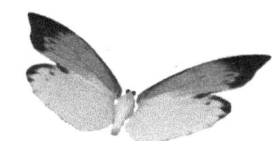

Doctors and Specialists

Primary Doctor		
Name of Practice	Phone Number	
Address		
City	State	Zip Code

Allergies to medications and food:

_____

_____

_____

_____

Specialists

- ☐ Cardiologist
- ☐ Endocrinologist
- ☐ Podiatrist
- ☐ Psychiatrist
- ☐ Other_____

- ☐ Oncologist
- ☐ Nephrologist
- ☐ Pulmonologist
- ☐ Orthopedic

_____

Doctor's Name		Type of Specialty	
Name of Practice		Phone Number	
Address			
City		State	Zip Code

Notes regarding this doctor / specialist:

_____

_____

_____

Doctor's Name		Type of Specialty	
Name of Practice		Phone Number	
Address			
City		State	Zip Code

Notes regarding this doctor / specialist:

_____

_____

_____

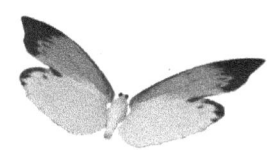

Doctor's Name	Type of Specialty	
Name of Practice	Phone Number	
Address		
City	State	Zip Code

Notes regarding this doctor / specialist:

_____

_____

_____

Doctor's Name	Type of Specialty	
Name of Practice	Phone Number	
Address		
City	State	Zip Code

Notes regarding this doctor / specialist:

_____

_____

_____

Doctor's Name	Type of Specialty	
Name of Practice	Phone Number	
Address		
City	State	Zip Code

Notes regarding this doctor / specialist:

_____

_____

_____

Doctor's Name	Type of Specialty	
Name of Practice	Phone Number	
Address		
City	State	Zip Code

Notes regarding this doctor / specialist:

_____

_____

_____

    ME: Facts and Forecasts

HOSPITAL

Name of Hospital	Phone Number	
Address		
City	State	Zip Code

Prosthesis / removable devices / non-removable devices

- ☐ Pace maker
- ☐ Contact Lenses / Glasses
- ☐ Hearing Aides
- ☐ Insulin Pump
- ☐ Braces (location) _____
- ☐ Other _____

Other Assisting Devices and Aides

- ☐ Wheelchair
- ☐ Walker
- ☐ Cane
- ☐ Other _____

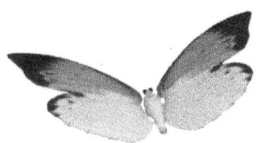

Surgeries I have had:

Date	Type of Surgery	Hospital	Doctor
Date	Type of Surgery	Hospital	Doctor
Date	Type of Surgery	Hospital	Doctor
Date	Type of Surgery	Hospital	Doctor
Date	Type of Surgery	Hospital	Doctor
Date	Type of Surgery	Hospital	Doctor
Date	Type of Surgery	Hospital	Doctor
Date	Type of Surgery	Hospital	Doctor
Date	Type of Surgery	Hospital	Doctor
Date	Type of Surgery	Hospital	Doctor
Date	Type of Surgery	Hospital	Doctor

Notes regarding surgeries:

_____

_____

_____

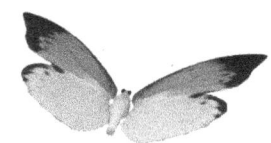

Medication Chart

Include all Prescription and Over the Counter medications:

Date	Name			
Medication, Strength, Dosage	☐ Breakfast	☐ Lunch	☐ Dinner	
Medication, Strength, Dosage	☐ Breakfast	☐ Lunch	☐ Dinner	
Medication, Strength, Dosage	☐ Breakfast	☐ Lunch	☐ Dinner	
Medication, Strength, Dosage	☐ Breakfast	☐ Lunch	☐ Dinner	
Medication, Strength, Dosage	☐ Breakfast	☐ Lunch	☐ Dinner	
Medication, Strength, Dosage	☐ Breakfast	☐ Lunch	☐ Dinner	
Medication, Strength, Dosage	☐ Breakfast	☐ Lunch	☐ Dinner	
Medication, Strength, Dosage	☐ Breakfast	☐ Lunch	☐ Dinner	
Medication, Strength, Dosage	☐ Breakfast	☐ Lunch	☐ Dinner	
Medication, Strength, Dosage	☐ Breakfast	☐ Lunch	☐ Dinner	

Location where I keep my medication: _____

I take my medication:

☐ by myself ☐ with assistance from my family ☐ with assistance from facility staff

PHARMACY

Name of Pharmacy	Phone Number	
Address		
City	State	Zip Code

MAIL ORDER PHARMACY

Name of Pharmacy	Phone Number	
Address		
City	State	Zip Code

PRESCRIPTION DRUG COVERAGE

Insurance Company	
Policy Number	Group Number
Phone or other contact number	
Responsible Party	

Other medical information (including diagnoses, conditions, ailments, etc.) and Special Instructions:

_____

_____

_____

_____

_____

_____

_____

_____

_____

_____

_____

_____

_____

_____

DENTAL CARE

I wear dentures	Yes ☐	No ☐	
I have other dental appliances	Yes ☐	No ☐	
I have dental insurance	Yes ☐	No ☐	

Dentist's Name		
Name of Practice	Phone Number	
Address		
City	State	Zip Code
Insurance Company	Policy Number	
Responsible Party	Group Number	

Notes regarding this dentist:

_____

_____

_____

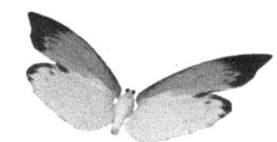

VISION CARE

I wear glasses	Yes ☐	No ☐
I wear contacts	Yes ☐	No ☐
I have had Lasik eye surgery	Yes ☐	No ☐
I have vision insurance	Yes ☐	No ☐
I have an eye care specialist	Yes ☐	No ☐

Eye Doctor's Name		
Name of Practice	Phone Number	
Address		
City	State	Zip Code
Insurance Company	Policy Number	
Responsible Party	Group Number	

Notes regarding this eye doctor:

_____

_____

_____

Specialist's Name		
Name of Practice	Phone Number	
Address		
City	State	Zip Code
Insurance Company	Policy Number	
Responsible Party	Group Number	

Notes regarding this doctor/specialist:

_____

_____

_____

Other Important Medical Information (i.e., dietary issues, etc.):

_____

_____

_____

_____

_____

_____

_____

_____

_____

_____

ME: FACTS AND FORECASTS

ME: THE FACTS

FINANCIAL INFORMATION

Financial information is everywhere. Much of your financial information is protected — as it should be — from identity theft, fraud, etc. Financial information includes not only assets in your possession, but also your right to future monies, your debt (both current and long term), and your planned estate.

Knowing the existence of such information can be priceless (pardon the pun) and save your financial life in times of crisis — or even in daily matters.

The following section does **not** have space for you to record the **amount** or **value** of your assets — only what they are and where they are located. Without a listing or other obvious paperwork, locating your assets can be a time-consuming task — with the risk that all your property may not be recovered. The existence of these assets can help to identify what is rightly yours and assist in its protection.

Although this is the largest portion of this book, it is broken down into the following sections: Assets, Income, Liabilities and Expenses, and Service Providers. Fill in as much information as you know on any one item. Be sure to identify if any accounts are held "jointly" or by more than one person.

FINANCIAL INFORMATION - ASSETS

I have savings account(s)	Yes ☐	No ☐
I have checking account(s)	Yes ☐	No ☐
I have Certificate(s) of Deposit	Yes ☐	No ☐
I have brokerage account(s)	Yes ☐	No ☐
I have retirement account(s)	Yes ☐	No ☐
Pension(s)	Yes ☐	No ☐
IRA's	Yes ☐	No ☐
I have annuity contracts	Yes ☐	No ☐
I have life insurance policies	Yes ☐	No ☐
I have a house	Yes ☐	No ☐
Other real estate	Yes ☐	No ☐
I have other property	Yes ☐	No ☐
Car	Yes ☐	No ☐
Motorcycle	Yes ☐	No ☐
Boat, RV, etc.	Yes ☐	No ☐
Antiques / Artwork	Yes ☐	No ☐
Jewelry	Yes ☐	No ☐

I have a safe	Yes ☐	No ☐
I have a safety deposit box	Yes ☐	No ☐
I have a trust fund	Yes ☐	No ☐

Relevant documents are located in:

_____

_____

I have other assets (businesses, etc.)　Yes ☐　　No ☐

Type and description:

_____

_____

_____

_____

_____

_____

_____

_____

_____

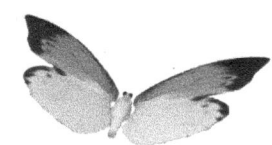

Savings Accounts and Checking Accounts

Location (Name of Bank or Financial Institution)		
Address		
City	State	Zip Code
Type of Account	Account Number	

Notes regarding this account:

_____

_____

_____

Location (Name of Bank or Financial Institution)		
Address		
City	State	Zip Code
Type of Account	Account Number	

Notes regarding this account:

_____

_____

_____

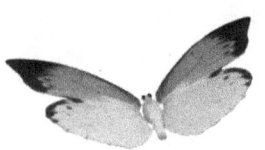

Location (Name of Bank or Financial Institution)		
Address		
City	State	Zip Code
Type of Account	Account Number	

Notes regarding this account:

_____

_____

_____

Location (Name of Bank or Financial Institution)		
Address		
City	State	Zip Code
Type of Account	Account Number	

Notes regarding this account:

_____

_____

_____

CERTIFICATES OF DEPOSIT

Location (Name of Bank or Financial Institution)		
Address		
City	State	Zip Code
Type of Account	Account Number	

Notes regarding this account:

_____

_____

_____

Location (Name of Bank or Financial Institution)		
Address		
City	State	Zip Code
Type of Account	Account Number	

Notes regarding this account:

_____

_____

_____

BROKERAGE ACCOUNTS

Location (Name of Bank or Financial Institution)		
Address		
City	State	Zip Code
Type of Account	Account Number	

Notes regarding this account:

_____

_____

_____

Location (Name of Bank or Financial Institution)		
Address		
City	State	Zip Code
Type of Account	Account Number	

Notes regarding this account:

_____

_____

_____

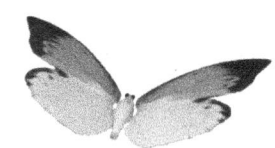

Retirement (Pension) Accounts

Location (Name of Bank or Financial Institution)		
Address		
City	State	Zip Code
Type of Account	Account Number	

Notes regarding this account:

_____

_____

_____

Location (Name of Bank or Financial Institution)		
Address		
City	State	Zip Code
Type of Account	Account Number	

Notes regarding this account:

_____

_____

_____

INDIVIDUAL RETIREMENT ACCOUNTS (IRAs)

Location (Name of Bank or Financial Institution)		
Address		
City	State	Zip Code
Type of Account	Account Number	

Notes regarding this account:

_____

_____

_____

Location (Name of Bank or Financial Institution)		
Address		
City	State	Zip Code
Type of Account	Account Number	

Notes regarding this account:

_____

_____

_____

ANNUITY

Location (Name of Insurance Company or Financial Institution)		
Address		
City	State	Zip Code
Type of Account	Account Number	

Notes regarding this account:

_____

_____

_____

Location (Name of Insurance Company or Financial Institution)		
Address		
City	State	Zip Code
Type of Account	Account Number	

Notes regarding this account:

_____

_____

_____

LIFE INSURANCE

Location (Name of Insurance Company or Financial Institution)		
Address		
City	State	Zip Code
Type of Account	Account Number	

Notes regarding this account:

_____

_____

_____

Location (Name of Insurance Company or Financial Institution)		
Address		
City	State	Zip Code
Type of Account	Account Number	

Notes regarding this account:

_____

_____

_____

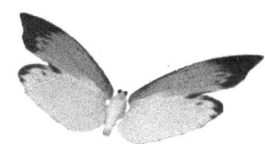

HOUSE AND OTHER REAL ESTATE PROPERTY

Address		
City	State	Zip Code
Location of Deed		
Mortgage Lender	Account Number	

Notes regarding this asset:

_____

_____

_____

Address		
City	State	Zip Code
Location of Deed		
Mortgage Lender	Account Number	

Notes regarding this asset:

_____

_____

_____

CARS AND MOTORCYCLES

Make		Model	Year
Address			Color
City		State	Zip Code
Location of Keys		Location of Title or Deed	

Notes regarding this asset:

_____

_____

_____

Make		Model	Year
Address			Color
City		State	Zip Code
Location of Keys		Location of Title or Deed	

Notes regarding this asset:

_____

_____

_____

Boats, RVs, Etc.

Make		Model	Year
Address			Color
City		State	Zip Code
Location of Keys		Location of Title or Deed	

Notes regarding this asset:

_____

_____

_____

Make		Model	Year
Address			Color
City		State	Zip Code
Location of Keys		Location of Title or Deed	

Notes regarding this asset:

_____

_____

_____

Other vehicles information or special instructions:

_____

_____

_____

_____

_____

_____

_____

_____

_____

_____

_____

_____

_____

_____

_____

_____

_____

_____

OTHER ASSETS — ANTIQUES, ART, JEWELRY, ETC.

Location		
Address		
City	State	Zip Code
Type of Asset	Location of Any Paperwork	

Notes regarding this asset:

_____

_____

_____

Location		
Address		
City	State	Zip Code
Type of Asset	Location of Any Paperwork	

Notes regarding this asset:

_____

_____

_____

Location		
Address		
City	State	Zip Code
Type of Asset	Location of Any Paperwork	

Notes regarding this asset:

_____

_____

_____

Location		
Address		
City	State	Zip Code
Type of Asset	Location of Any Paperwork	

Notes regarding this asset:

_____

_____

_____

  ME: FACTS AND FORECASTS

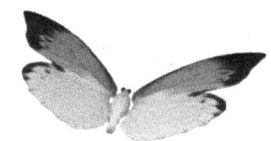

SAFE

Location (Bank, House, etc.)		
Address		
City	State	Zip Code
Location of Key	Other code number	

Notes regarding this safe:

_____

_____

SAFETY DEPOSIT BOX

Location (Bank, House, etc.)		
Address		
City	State	Zip Code
Location of Key	Other code number	

Notes regarding this safety deposit box:

_____

_____

Other Assets or Special Instructions:

_____

_____

_____

_____

_____

_____

_____

_____

_____

_____

_____

_____

_____

_____

_____

_____

_____

_____

_____

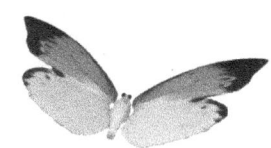

FINANCIAL INFORMATION — INCOME

I am currently employed   Yes ☐   No ☐

    I receive my salary by   Check ☐   Direct Deposit ☐

I receive a pension/retirement   Yes ☐   No ☐

    I receive payment by   Check ☐   Direct Deposit ☐

I receive social security   Yes ☐   No ☐

    I receive payment by   Check ☐   Direct Deposit ☐

I have other income (cash, dividends, etc.)   Yes ☐   No ☐

    I receive payment by   Check ☐   Direct Deposit ☐

    Frequency _____

    Type _____

I have a deferred compensation plan   Yes ☐   No ☐

CURRENT EMPLOYER

Employer		
Address		
City	State	Zip Code
Position	Phone Number	

Notes regarding this employer:

_____

_____

PENSION DISTRIBUTIONS OR
DEFERRED COMPENSATION

Former Employer		
Address		
City	State	Zip Code
Contact Person	Phone Number	

Notes regarding this:

_____

_____

Former Employer		
Address		
City	State	Zip Code
Contact Person	Phone Number	

Notes regarding this:

_____

_____

Former Employer		
Address		
City	State	Zip Code
Contact Person	Phone Number	

Notes regarding this:

_____

_____

FINANCIAL INFORMATION —
LIABILITIES & EXPENSES

My expense payments are:

☐ Mortgage   ☐ Rent

☐ Line of Credit / Second Mortgage

☐ Home Owner's Association Dues

☐ Home Owner's Insurance   ☐ Renter's Insurance

☐ Insurance for specific assets

☐ Car Payment   ☐ Car Insurance

☐ Other vehicle payment

☐ Credit Cards

My utility and other housekeeping expenses are:

☐ Electric   ☐ Gas   ☐ Water

☐ Phone   ☐ Cell Phone

☐ Cable television ☐ Computer / Internet provider

☐ Yard care   ☐ Housecleaning

☐ Service contracts — appliances, pool, etc.

My other expenses are:

_____

_____

_____

_____

_____

_____

I pay my bills:

☐ by myself   ☐ with help from others _____

My bills are paid:

☐ by Check   ☐ Electronically   ☐ by Credit Card

If paid electronically, from what account?

_____

_____

If paid by credit card, from what account?

_____

_____

Location of most recent years' tax returns:

_____

_____

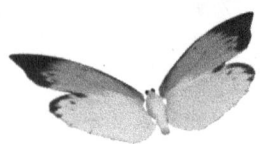

MORTGAGE

Location (Name of Bank or Financial Institution)		
Property Address		
Address		
City	State	Zip Code
Method of Payment	Account Number	

Notes regarding this account:

_____

_____

LINE OF CREDIT / SECOND MORTGAGE

Location (Name of Bank or Financial Institution)		
Address		
City	State	Zip Code
Method of Payment	Account Number	

Notes regarding this account:

_____

_____

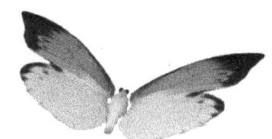

HOME OWNER'S ASSOCIATION

Location (Name of Bank or Financial Institution)		
Address		
City	State	Zip Code
Method of Payment	Account Number	

Notes regarding this account:

_____

_____

RENT

Landlord		
Property Address		
Address		
City	State	Zip Code
Method of Payment	Account Number	

Notes regarding this account:

_____

_____

Home Owner's / Renter's Insurance Payments

Property Address		
Insurance Provider		
Address		
City	State	Zip Code
Method of Payment	Policy Number	

Notes regarding this policy:

_____

_____

Property Address		
Insurance Provider		
Address		
City	State	Zip Code
Method of Payment	Policy Number	

Notes regarding this policy:

_____

_____

INSURANCE FOR SPECIFIC ASSETS

Type of Asset		
Insurance Provider		
Address		
City	State	Zip Code
Method of Payment	Policy Number	

Notes regarding this policy:

_____

_____

Type of Asset		
Insurance Provider		
Address		
City	State	Zip Code
Method of Payment	Policy Number	

Notes regarding this policy:

_____

_____

Car and Other Vehicle Payments

Make	Model	Year
Location (Name of Bank or Financial Institution)		
Address		
City	State	Zip Code
Method of Payment	Account Number	

Notes regarding this account:

_____

_____

Make	Model	Year
Location (Name of Bank or Financial Institution)		
Address		
City	State	Zip Code
Method of Payment	Account Number	

Notes regarding this account:

_____

_____

CAR AND OTHER VEHICLE INSURANCE

Car or other vehicle		
Insurance Provider		
Address		
City	State	Zip Code
Method of Payment	Policy Number	

Notes regarding this policy:

_____

_____

Car or other vehicle		
Insurance Provider		
Address		
City	State	Zip Code
Method of Payment	Policy Number	

Notes regarding this policy:

_____

_____

CREDIT CARDS

Credit Card Company		
Address		
City	State	Zip Code
Method of Payment	Account Number	

Notes regarding this account:

_____

_____

Credit Card Company		
Address		
City	State	Zip Code
Method of Payment	Account Number	

Notes regarding this account:

_____

_____

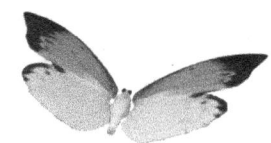

Electric

Utility Provider		
Address		
City	State	Zip Code
Method of Payment	Account Number	

Notes regarding this account:

_____

_____

Gas

Utility Provider		
Address		
City	State	Zip Code
Method of Payment	Account Number	

Notes regarding this account:

_____

_____

WATER

Utility Provider		
Address		
City	State	Zip Code
Method of Payment	Account Number	

Notes regarding this account:

_____

_____

PHONE

Utility Provider		
Address		
City	State	Zip Code
Method of Payment	Account Number	

Notes regarding this account:

_____

_____

CELL PHONE

Utility Provider		
Address		
City	State	Zip Code
Method of Payment	Account Number	

Notes regarding this account:

_____

_____

CABLE TELEVISION/SATELLITE/DISH NETWORK

Utility Provider		
Address		
City	State	Zip Code
Method of Payment	Account Number	

Notes regarding this account:

_____

_____

Computer/Internet Provider

Utility Provider		
Address		
City	State	Zip Code
Method of Payment	Account Number	

Notes regarding this account:

_____

_____

Yard Care

Provider		
Address		
City	State	Zip Code
Method of Payment	Account Number	

Notes regarding this account:

_____

_____

HOUSECLEANING

Utility Provider		
Address		
City	State	Zip Code
Method of Payment	Account Number	

Notes regarding this account:

_____

_____

SERVICE CONTRACTS (APPLIANCES, POOL, ETC.)

Provider		
Address		
City	State	Zip Code
Method of Payment	Account Number	

Notes regarding this account:

_____

_____

OTHER

Utility Provider		
Address		
City	State	Zip Code
Method of Payment	Account Number	

Notes regarding this account:

_____

_____

Provider		
Address		
City	State	Zip Code
Method of Payment	Account Number	

Notes regarding this account:

_____

_____

ACCOUNTANT

Accountant's Name		
Name of Firm	Phone Number	
Address		
City	State	Zip Code

Notes regarding this provider:

_____

_____

ATTORNEY

Attorney's Name		
Name of Firm	Phone Number	
Address		
City	State	Zip Code

Notes regarding this provider:

_____

_____

FINANCIAL ADVISOR

Advisor's Name		
Name of Firm	Phone Number	
Address		
City	State	Zip Code

Notes regarding this provider:

_____

_____

OTHER PROVIDER

Provider's Name	Type of Provider	
Name of Firm	Phone Number	
Address		
City	State	Zip Code

Notes regarding this provider:

_____

_____

Additional notes regarding Assets, Expenses, etc.:

_____

_____

_____

_____

_____

_____

_____

_____

_____

_____

_____

_____

_____

_____

_____

_____

_____

_____

_____

_____

_____

ME: FACTS AND FORECASTS

ME: MY FORECASTS

MY FORECAST UPON DISABILITY

HEALTH CARE MATTERS

FINANCIAL AFFAIRS

MY FORECAST UPON DEATH

MY BODY

MY ESTATE

ME: MY FORECASTS

MY FORECAST UPON DISABILITY

For most of us, we think we are either going to be alive or dead—no one ever contemplates any other alternatives. However, statistics show that almost 90% of people die only after suffering from a long term illness. If this is your case, what are your forecasts for this time? What are your wishes? What choices would you make? Most of us have something or someone in mind — make your requests here.

HEALTHCARE MATTERS

This section of the book assists you in telling what your preferences would be in the event something happens to you and you need support with your day to day living and medical care. Where would you want to live? Who would you want to help you?

Financial affairs

This section provides a place for you to identify who you would want to handle your financial matters.

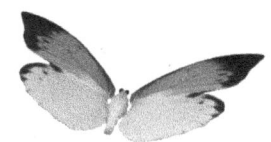

HEALTH CARE MATTERS

I have a Power of Attorney for Health Care Matters

Yes ☐   No ☐

Relevant documents are located in:

_____

_____

I have Advanced Directives for Healthcare

Yes ☐   No ☐

Relevant documents are located in:

_____

_____

I have a Legal Guardian for my person

Yes ☐   No ☐

Relevant Court documents are located in:

_____

_____

Power of Attorney / Legal Guardian	Phone Number	
Address		
City	State	Zip Code

My preference for living arrangements when I am disabled is:

☐ Live at home with assistance from relatives

☐ Live at home with assistance from private nursing, etc.

☐ Live at an assisted living facility

☐ Live at a long term care facility (nursing home)

My preference for Activities of Daily Living support when I am disabled is (bathing, toileting, dressing):

☐ Assistance from relatives

☐ Assistance from private nurse, etc.

☐ Assistance from facility staff

My preference for Instrumental Activities of Daily Living support when I am disabled is (managing finances, shopping, laundry, administering medication, coordinating medical care, arranging transportation, cleaning the house):

☐ Assistance from relatives

☐ Assistance from outside service including private nurse, etc.

☐ Assistance from facility staff

My preference for feeding support when I am disabled is:

☐ Assistance from relatives

☐ Assistance from private nurse, etc.

☐ Assistance from facility staff

If I live in a facility, I would like:

- ☐ A private room
- ☐ A shared room
- ☐ A private nurse
- ☐ A nurse that speaks another language: _____
- ☐ A facility near my family
- ☐ A facility near where I live now

Things I want with me in my room are:

_____

_____

_____

_____

_____

My other wishes should I become disabled:

_____

_____

_____

_____

_____

_____

_____

FINANCIAL MATTERS

I have a Power of Attorney for my Financial Affairs

Yes ☐   No ☐

Relevant documents are located in:

_____

_____

I have a Legal Guardian for my Estate

Yes ☐   No ☐

Relevant Court papers are located in:

_____

_____

Power of Attorney / Legal Guardian	Phone Number	
Address		
City	State	Zip Code

My other wishes regarding my finances when I become disabled are:

_____

_____

_____

_____

_____

_____

_____

_____

ME: FACTS AND FORECASTS

ME: MY FORECASTS

MY FORECAST UPON DEATH

Not many of us like to think about death — whether it's our own or someone we love. Yet, there is no denying it — it happens to all of us eventually. So when your time comes to leave this world — in whatever manner and at whatever time that may be — what is your forecast, your wishes, for your body and your estate?

MY BODY

In most instances, the remaining family members make decisions regarding how and where their loved ones will be prepared for burial. However, letting your family know ahead of time can ease the pain that everyone shares when that time is upon us. The following pages help you communicate your desires for those important end-of-life decisions, as well as your preferences regarding your body, your funeral, your burial, and even your obituary.

MY ESTATE

Many of us have heard of estate planning — although you may or may not have done any. In this section, you can identify who and where any estate information is kept, and provide any additional insights you want to share. You may also choose to write some of your legacies and remembrances.

MY BODY

DO NOT RESUSCITATE (DNR)?

Yes ☐   No ☐

LIFE SUPPORT

I DO want the following Life Support systems

☐ Feeding tube / nutritional therapy

☐ Medication therapy

☐ Oxygen therapy / Respirator

Signature _____

Date _____

My preference would be to have:

- ☐ Palliative Care

- ☐ Hospice Care

    - ☐ At home

    - ☐ In a facility

        - ☐ In a facility near family

        - ☐ In a facility near my home

ME: FACTS AND FORECASTS

My End of Life Decisions about my Body

I want:

☐ To be Buried

☐ To be Cremated

☐ To have my organs / body donated

☐ Other_____

Burial Plot / Niche

I have already purchased a plot or niche:

Yes ☐   No ☐   Preference indicated below ☐

Location		
Address		
City	State	Zip Code
Location of Paperwork		

Notes regarding my burial:

_____

_____

_____

_____

RELIGIOUS PREFERENCES

I have a religious preference for the preparation of my body:

Yes ☐   No ☐

Religion_____

Special Instructions:

_____

_____

_____

_____

_____

_____

_____

_____

ORGAN DONATION PREFERENCES

Special Instructions for organ/body donation:

_____

_____

_____

_____

_____

FUNERAL HOME

I have made arrangements with a funeral home:

Yes ☐   No ☐

Funeral Home	Phone Number	
Address		
City	State	Zip Code
Location of paperwork		

Special Instructions:

_____

_____

_____

_____

_____

FUNERAL PREFERENCES

I want to have a funeral service:

Yes ☐   No ☐

I want the following people to be notified of the service:

☐ Family only

☐ Family and Friends

☐ No preference

I have a religious preference for my funeral service and burial:

Yes ☐   No ☐

Religion_____

Special Instructions:

_____

_____

_____

_____

_____

_____

_____

_____

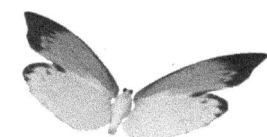

OBITUARY PREFERENCES

I have written my obituary:

Yes ☐   No ☐

My obituary is located _____

_____

I want my obituary provided to the following papers / places:

_____

_____

_____

_____

_____

_____

ME: FACTS AND FORECASTS

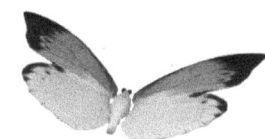

MY ESTATE

I have a Will:

   Yes ☐   No ☐

Relevant documents are located _____

Executor of Will		
Name of firm (if any)	Phone Number	
Address		
City	State	Zip Code

Others who have copies of my will:

_____

_____

_____

_____

BENEFICIARIES

I have beneficiary designations for the following:

- ☐ Pension benefits
- ☐ Brokerage accounts
- ☐ Life Insurance
- ☐ Annuity Contracts
- ☐ Other _____

Documentation for beneficiary designations is located:

For Pension benefits _____ _____

_____

For Brokerage accounts _____

_____

For Life Insurance accounts _____

_____

For Annuity Contracts _____

_____

For Other accounts _____

_____

_____

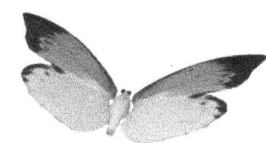

My Special Wishes and Legacies

My last three wishes are:

_____

_____

_____

_____

_____

I want to be remembered for:

_____

_____

_____

_____

My additional wishes and legacies are:

_____

_____

_____

_____

_____

_____

_____

Appendices

Glossary of Terms

For More Information

ME: Facts and Forecasts

GLOSSARY OF TERMS

Activities of Daily Living (ADLs)

Everyday functions and activities that people usually do help. These include dressing, eating, bathing, toileting, transferring and continence.

Advanced Directives

An advance health care directive, also known as living will, personal directive, advance directive, or advance decision, are instructions given by individuals specifying what actions should be taken for their health in the event that they are no longer able to make decisions due to illness or incapacity. The Advanced Directive appoints a person to make such decisions on their behalf.

Annuity

A contract sold by an insurance company designed to provide payments at specified intervals.

Assets

Any property owned by a person.

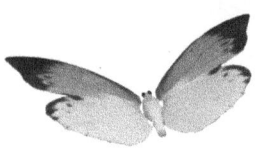

Beneficiary

A person or group designated as the recipient of funds or other property under a will.

Brokerage Account

An account held at a financial institution that allows you to purchase stocks, bonds, mutual funds, and other investments by paying professionals to buy or sell these items on your behalf.

Burial Plot

A piece of land that is purchased from a cemetery for the purpose of burying a loved one's body or ashes.

Burial Niche

A shelf-like space in a mausoleum structure used for the inurnment of cremated remains. Urns are placed in these niches as a final resting place for cremated remains. Niches come in different sizes.

Cardiologist

Doctor specializing in the heartthat diagnose and treat diseases and cardiovascular diseases.

Certificate of Deposit (CD)

Similar to a savings account, except that the CD has a specific, fixed term (often three months, six months, or one to five years), and, usually, a fixed interest rate. It is intended that the CD be held until maturity, at which time the money may be withdrawn together with the accrued interest.

Deferred Compensation

An arrangement in which a portion of an employee's income is received at a date after which that income is actually earned.

Dividends

Money paid to shareholders of a company.

Endocrinologist

Doctor specializing in the glands and hormones of the body.

Estate

Property, both real and personal, tangible and intangible, and includes anything that may be subject to ownership.

Executor

Person named to carry out the provisions of a Will.

Hospice Care

A nursing home or service that specializes in caring for the terminally ill.

Immunologists

Doctor who specializes in the treatment of diseases of the immune system.

IRA

Individual Retirement Account.

Instrumental Activities of Daily Living (IADLs)

Tasks that, in addition to activities of daily living, you must be able to perform in order to live independently (without

the assistance or substantial supervision of another person). Examples include grocery shopping, meal preparation, using the telephone, laundry, light housekeeping, bill paying, and managing your medications.

Intestate

Dying without a legal will.

Irrevocable Trust

A trust that, once executed, cannot be revoked or changed without the consent of the beneficiary.

Legacy

Anything handed down from the past.

Legal Guardian

A person who has the legal authority (and the corresponding duty) to care for the personal and property of another person, called the Ward. Usually, a person has the status of guardian because the ward is incapable of caring for his or her own interests due to infancy, incapacity or disability. Courts generally have the power to appoint a guardian for an individual in need of special protection.

Liability

A debt or financial obligation.

Living Trust

A trust created during someone's lifetime to hold assets during that person's lifetime, thereby removing those assets from probate at death. A living trust can be either revocable

or irrevocable. It avoids probate and therefore gets assets distributed significantly faster than a will. Assets that a person wants to move to a living trust, such as real estate and bank or brokerage accounts, must be retitled so that the trust becomes the owner.

Living Will

A legal document in which a person specifies which life-prolonging medical measures he or she does, and does not, want to be taken if he or she becomes terminally ill or incapacitated.

Long Term Care

A variety of services provided over an extended period of time to people who need help to perform normal activities of daily living because of cognitive impairment or loss of muscular strength or control. Care may include rehabilitative therapies, skilled nursing, and palliative care, as well as supervision and a wide range of supportive personal care and social services. Long-term care can be provided at home, or in a facility, including nursing homes and assisted living facilities.

Medicaid

A joint federal/state program that pays for health care for individuals and families with low incomes or very high medical bills relative to their income and assets. Coverage and eligibility requirements vary from state-to-state. Medicaid is the primary payer of nursing home care.

Medicare

The federal program that provides hospital and medical care to people age 65 or older, and to some younger people who are very ill or disabled. Benefits for nursing home and short-term home health services are limited and are generally available only to people while they are recovering from an acute illness. Coverage is restricted to medical care, and does not include custodial care at home or in nursing homes.

Nephrologist

Doctor specializing in the functions of the kidney.

Neurologist

Doctor specializing in the functions of the nervous system (i.e., brain, spinal cord and nerves).They treat conditions like seizures, strokes, Parkinson's, Alzheimer's, etc.

Obituary

A notice of the death of a person.

Oncologist

Doctor specializing in cancer.

Ophthalmologist

Doctor specializing in diseases of the eye.

Orthopedic

Doctor specializing in correcting discomfort of spine, joints and skeletal system of the human body.

Palliative Care

Service designed to relieve or lessen pain, disease, etc., without curing.

Podiatrist

Doctor specializing in foot disorders.

Power of Attorney

Authority to act for another person in legal or financial matters.

Prosthesis

An artificial part.

Psychiatrist

Doctor specializing in diagnosis and treatment of mental disorders.

Pulmonologist

Doctor specializing in diseases of the lungs.

Revocable Trust

A trust in which a Grantor reserves the right to revoke or change. To protect the final wishes of the Grantor, a trust can become irrevocable upon the death of the Grantor.

Resuscitate

To revive, especially from apparent death.

Rheumatologist

Doctor that specialize in the treatment of allergic conditions and autoimmune disorders.

Skilled Nursing Facility (SNF)

A nursing facility (in most cases, a nursing home; sometimes a special unit inside a hospital) that has been certified by Medicare, with the staff and equipment to give skilled nursing care and/or skilled rehabilitation services and other related health services.

Trust

A fund administered separately and used for specific purposes.

Urologists

Doctor who specializes in the urinary system.

Will

Otherwise known as a Last Will and Testament; a written document through which a person disposes of property after death.

FOR MORE INFORMATION

To learn more, please visit our Web site and
contact us at our headquarters near Chicago, Illinois.

Customized Caring, Inc.
901 Indigo Court
Hanover Park, Illinois 60133
www.customizedcaring.com

ME: Facts and Forecasts

www.ingramcontent.com/pod-product-compliance
Lightning Source LLC
Chambersburg PA
CBHW080515110426
42742CB00017B/3123